LITTLE

BLACK

GIRLS

H M VAUGHN

authorHOUSE®

AuthorHouse™
1663 Liberty Drive
Bloomington, IN 47403
www.authorhouse.com
Phone: 833-262-8899

Published by AuthorHouse 09/01/2020

ISBN: 978-1-7283-7082-8 (sc)
ISBN: 978-1-7283-7305-8 (e)

Hello Beautiful

Black Girls!!!

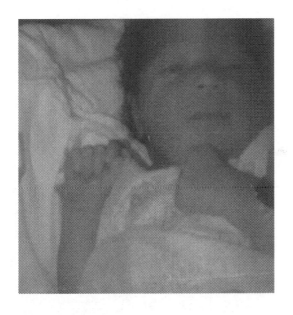

You are very important to our society.

Dark Black, Light Black

and mixed with Black

You are special!!!

You are wanted!!!

You are LOVED!!!

Black girls wear your skin proudly, wear your smile proudly, wear your hair proudly, and wear yourself proudly.

So pretty black girls don't focus on your skin color be thankful that you don't have to spend money on a tanning bed. Put on your skin moisturizer and glow. Your dark black, light black and mixed black skin is standing out and shining like the sun, so never let someone tell you that your Black is not beautiful.

Black is Beautiful and just like wearing clothes when things seem to stick to black remember that your black is beautiful and you should let your black stick to you.

And we all know black goes with everything!!!

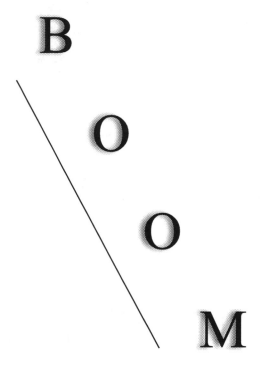

Beautiful Black girls

You should be able to wear your natural hair without feeling bad about having long or short hair. It's about being comfortable with yourself and knowing you.

You know what hairstyles go with your face and what doesn't, how to be creative and still have your own identity.

No matter what our skin color is we all wear wigs, weaves, and hair extensions. So, by allowing anyone to make you feel bad about yourself should be nonexistent.

Beautiful Black girls!!!

What should stick to you?

Your smile should always stick.

Your talent should always stick.

Your confidence should always stick.

So you can show your beauty all of the time.

This is what sticks to me and I hope that you allow it to stick to you too!!!

Your black is special because when you walk and talk people pay attention no matter if they are thinking positive or negative don't be sad or confused always know your black is just for you!!!

I am a mother of three different skin toned black girls two of them had the same problems in school with their skin tones different shades same problem because of their color.

But I taught them how to stay focused, know who they are, and who they want to be, as long as it's positive you are winning because you are you so always show your black in a positive manner.

Black girls you are on a higher level.

"Why do I say that beautiful black girls"? It's because you have the color you have the knowledge so what others think should not matter. Be you a beautiful black girl.

Black girls what do you see when you look in the mirror?

_____

_____

Always look for the positive you. Why? Because in every area of your life you are going to improve so, I say improve in your positive reflection and never the negative reflection.

Beautiful Black Girl

Slide your favorite picture of you in the slot above and you can change it every month or year to see your growth, your black beauty.

Black girl's please stay focus on not just the outside beauty but the inside as well. So never allow someone to say your black is not beauty.

I know that it is hard a lot of times but when you are the ages 1-5, you look in the mirror and try to see yourself as your vision and focus becomes clear you are seeing you for the first time. Your site comprehending who you are as a little person and you continues to grow as you get older.

Beautiful Black girl's looking at yourself in the mirror as a teen.

I no longer want to match with this color... I don't want to put weave in my hair today... I know my black is beautiful with or without... So my beauty doesn't come from my clothes or my hair because, when I first looked in the mirror the first thing I seen is the skin I wear.

So no one can break me down with ignorant comments because no matter the color of my skin we all put on the same color of clothing and hair.

Black girls learn as you grow to not focus on just your skin color I cannot stress this enough because it's how you handle life situations in a certain manner we are not being judged by the color of our skin but what's within.

We are being tested on what positive things you/we do in the skin you/we wear.

Beautiful black girl's dress your mind and body with the best because you are strong and you are talented. Take time to get to know you. Block out whatever negative try to come in your life.

Be creative write your own saying here

_____

Be inspired by others but mostly be inspired by you!!!

My inspired saying is

I know who I am

_____

_____

_____

_____

_____

_____

I didn't know how to deal with certain things in school as a child. So when some people said you are pretty and others said you are pretty to be black and at that age it was confusing. But I had people in my life who explained the right and wrong ways to say things. So from that day forth I never saw myself as a blacky just a beautiful black girl.

So when I went to school and they would call me blacky

I would look in a mirror and I knew I was pretty and

not just my skin color. I was smart and as I got older I

became one of the popular kids and I am dark as heck.

So look at you, get to know you, and know

you don't stop at your skin color!!!

Beautiful Black girls

This is your page.

My name is

_____

And I am a beautiful black girl and I am going to encourage

myself to be:

_____

_____

_____

_____

Beautiful Black Girl's

Always dress and talk with class and respect. You can always get your point across when you have the correct knowledge.

This book is to inspire all of us and we are all here to be loved. So start loving yourselves with and without the dressings.

These are my daughters.

Gair

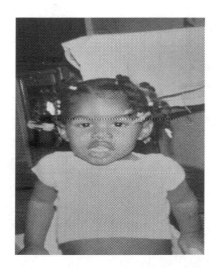

Niqua

This is my great grandmother who started us.

Beautiful Black girls remember it's not a compliment when someone says you're pretty to be a black girl or a mixed girl.

Say 'NO' I'm just BEAUTIFUL!!!

I thank everyone who helped me get this positive

motivational message out to our entire beautiful black girl's.

Stay Strong & Beautiful!!!

My Picture

Heidi Vaughn, writer of Little Black Girls

Printed in the United States
By Bookmasters